Merrill Wagner

Merrill Wagner

interview by
Ann Messner and William S. Bartman

essay by Lilly Wei

Published by
A.R.T. Press, New York
2003

Installation, May 2002
Art Resources Transfer, New York

Merrill Wagner
Interview: Merrill Wagner with Ann Messner and Bill Bartman
Essay: Lilly Wei
Editor: Bill Bartman
Copyeditors: Diane Mark-Walker and Richard G. Gallin
Design: Lautsen/Cossutta Design, Sierra Madre, Califonia
Production: Amanda Washburn, New York
Printing: Dr. Cantz'sche Druckerei, Germany
Photography: Brian Forrest, Cyrus Happy, Peter Mönning,
Joshua Nefsky, Nathan Rabin, Jeff Sturgess, Lynn Thompson,
Merrill Wagner

Distributor:
R.A.M. Publications + Distributions, Inc.
2525 Michigan Avenue, Bldg. #A2
Santa Monica, CA 90404
tel.: 310.453.0043
fax: 310.264.4888
e-mail: rampub@gte.net

ISBN 0-923183-31-0

cover and back flap:
Merrill Wagner painting in preparation for
Notes on Paint, 1978–79, Tacoma, Washington
Photographed by Cyrus Happy

Art Resources Transfer, Inc., is a nonprofit, tax-exempt organization
that was founded in 1987 to publish books on artists in which the
artist plays the central role in the development and production of
the actual book.

Contents

Red Roof, 1993
Oil, acrylic, slate, shingles
4 x 8 feet
installation view:
The Aldrich Museum of Contemporary Art, Ridgefield, Connecticut
January 1993

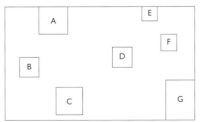

Slate Shingles/Cadmium Red Medium, 1993
(on exhibit adjacent to terrace in Sculpture Garden)

Oil Pastel	Oil Log (F)
	Marcal (E)
Acrylic Paint	Lascaux (B)
	Golden (D)
Oil Paint	Old Holland (G)
	Block (A)
	Seawright's Vermilion (C)

Introduction

Working on this book for the past two years with Merrill has been very much like the embodiment of her work and her concerns, i.e., very process oriented. Each step—whether editing the conversation, choosing the images, deciding on the format, or working with the writer—has involved a slow and thoughtful process. Nothing has been easy or without great deliberation. Creating the finished project is thus a cathartic event much like producing every one of our A.R.T. Press Books because the artist is a full partner in this collaboration. These books could not have been created without this partnership of artist, editor, writer, and designers. This is our first one-artist book since the publication of *The Portrait Speaks,* and it has allowed for the more intimate and complex understanding of the work of one artist. I had forgotten after the six years of working with Chuck Close and the twenty-seven other artists involved in that project how difficult it is for artists to participate in this kind of publishing endeavor—one where they have the final approval on all aspects of the project. In this case, it has allowed Merrill Wagner, who has been exhibiting and creating a vast and varied body of work for more than forty years, to look thoughtfully at all of her work that lends itself to this particular publishing process. From her own book projects to her recent designs for choreographer Molissa Fenley she defies categorizing, which allows for this book to follow her exploration of the complex and multilayered through lines of her very personal artistic journey.

Bill Bartman

Summer Studio, September 1985
Oil pastel, paints, soft pastel on cedar fence
4 x 4 feet

A Conversation between Merrill Wagner, Ann Messner, and Bill Bartman

17 West 16th Street, New York, Spring 2001

Ann Messner: You said that the aspect of time was perhaps something that you had been interested in earlier but not so much now, but that's not so.

Merrill Wagner: What I meant was at a certain point it interested me that there were different brands of paint that were the same color, but they all looked different, because they were different. For instance, if you go and buy cobalt blue in an art-supply store, and you get different brands of cobalt blue, you have all different kinds of colors.

Ann: This is a painter's nightmare.

Merrill: Yeah, a painter's nightmare.

Ann: But if it's real cobalt, then it would always look the same.

Merrill: You're right, but if you're making a painting with Winsor & Newton cobalt blue, and you say: "I've run out of paint—I need to get some more." And they say, "We don't have any more Winsor & Newton. How about Block?" Block cobalt blue will be a different shade from Winsor & Newton.

Bill Bartman: And it'll weather differently.

Merrill: Yeah.

Bill: Because time affects it differently.

Merrill: Yes. So it interested me that you could go and buy cobalt blue in all these different brands, and they would all be different colors. I thought I would like to make a painting with eight different brands of paint, with the same name color, and use them in a composition. Then I would place the painting outdoors and photograph it over a period of years.

I've still been photographing the projects that I started in 1983 for *Notes on Paint*. I tried to compose the painting so that it would look interesting over a long period of time as the colors changed outdoors. I used certain brands of paint that were most durable like Golden acrylic in parts of the composition so that the structure of the painting would hold up as it weathered.

But, you know, at first I didn't know what would do what. I knew that watercolor wouldn't last as long as acrylic, and so forth. I was interested in working on that sort of idea and I still am.

Bill: When you described it you said, "I want to make a painting with six different colors," which is fine. Then you said, "Of course, what I did was put it outside for fifteen years, and took pictures of it over the fifteen-year period." Then it wasn't just about the colors. The book is really about time and the passage of time.

Merrill: Well, that is the reason I made the book. I wouldn't otherwise have gone out and taken a photograph of the backyard, or of this landscape here, or of this fence and the water. The focus was the painting.

Bill: No, I understand that. But what ends up happening with the paint you've applied to a surface, is that the passage of time is like a microcosm of what would happen to, let's say, the Grand Canyon over a period of a thousand years. It's as if we could watch the earth change, as though the ocean were moving three or five feet.

Merrill: Yeah.

Bill: You can't do that. This is more than a lifetime. But you can actually describe a passage of time with these paintings.

Merrill: Yes.

Bill: And experience it.

Merrill: Yeah.

Bill: Because you see the seasons changing; you see the years changing.

Merrill: Right.

Ann: This aspect of time seems pervasive in the work; and especially with the perennial landscape paintings on canvas that you do all year round. With these perennial paintings, you made a comment about how the subject matter demands to be painted. Time is crucial, so that if you don't do it now, it's going to be gone, it will be too late. There's an urgency.

Merrill: If I see something that's really beautiful in nature, it makes me want to paint it immediately before the light or weather changes. I mostly paint from nature when the subject matter seems manageable in scale. Certain types of landscapes are intimate but I don't feel an intimacy in the kind of landscape where I grew up in Washington State.

I feel that in my large paintings there is a memory of the way the landscape is on the West Coast or the Rocky Mountains.

Ann: Like the steel paintings…

Merrill: Yeah.

Merrill: There are certain aspects of nature: flowers are intimate—you can pick them. And they're temporary. But there are other things, for instance, if you look at the ocean, or if you go to the desert. Or…

Bill: The night sky.

Merrill: Yeah. I mean, you can't change that.

Ann: And you can't have that same physical relationship with it.

Merrill: You can't influence it, anyway. It doesn't care about you. You just have to be there as a little observer. And I think the larger paintings—the steel paintings—are more about that kind of experience.

Ann: And so what about humor? When you documented the weathering of the yellow painting in your backyard in *Notes On Paint*—which is one of my favorite books—in the photographs there are dogs, and the dogs appear to weather along with the work.

Merrill: Well, they get older and older.

Ann: The framing of the painting is minimalist, the sequenced monochrome rectangle.

Ann Messner
Frogman, 1977
from "*Subway Stories*"

Photographed by Peter Mönning

That is what it is. You chose forms that are high, hierarchical, and modernist. Then, within this minimal form, in the photographs you choose to include the dogs and it's funny, really funny.

Merrill: *(laughs)*

Ann: Also, just the fact that the painting is getting weathered and older and older. In your calendar book from 1982 the painting that goes underwater in the lake appears and disappears, and it is at the mercy of what the water level is doing, and certainly has inherent humor. I also think it's very ingenious… as a solution. But what about this sense of humor?

Merrill: No, I photographed the dogs by accident as they were running past me. I tried to exclude them.

Ann: Well, you could have excluded them by locking them up in the house.

Merrill: Yes, but sometimes the dog would run up and just sort of pose, in this beautiful dog pose, and so I thought: Wow, if I took that picture! I got to like it when they would be there. There are no people in the photographs. There are no figures, but there are dogs. I hadn't thought about it—I hadn't thought about humans. I thought the dogs were funny too. In the book *Time and Materials* we put a picture of my dog Midnight, who was twenty years old, on the most important page, the first page, just by himself with no paint or anything like that. It had to do with time. I am interested in making visual jokes sometimes, but it just happens once in a while. I don't plan it, but it's good to catch it when it does.

from *A Calendar*
September 1982–December 1983
35 pages, color photographs throughout
8$^{1}/_{2}$ x 11 inches

Notes on Paint and *Time and Materials* measure the ability of artists' paint to withstand weather changes over years. Later books, *Painted Sun Trails* and *Oil and Water*, record shadows painted as I observed them moving across stones or boulders during the course of days and then seasons.

A Calendar
September 1982–December 1983
35 pages, color photographs throughout
8¹/₂ x 11 inches

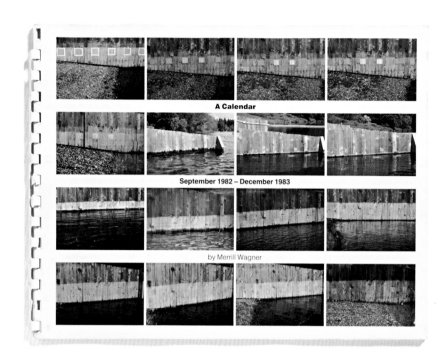

September 1982

The site of this project is a cedar fence running into the fresh water of Gravelly Lake near Tacoma, Washington. Six rectangles of yellow paint, nearly the same color, were applied to the fence, just below the high-water mark where the lake had risen during the preceding year. Two of the rectangles were painted with watercolor, two with tempera, and two with oil paint. One rectangle of each of the three pairs was applied directly onto the bare wood of the fence. The second rectangle of each pair was separated from the fence by three coats of Varathane, which sealed the wood before the paint was applied.

It was not known at the outset precisely how each of these small areas of color would tolerate the exposure to sun, wind, and water. Once the paint was laid down, nature was in control of the project.

Photographs were taken each month by Cyrus Happy from approximately the same view, as the lake rose during the winter months and receded the following summer. This passage of time is recorded in these pages as a sixteen-month calendar.

Notes on Paint, 1983–90
80 pages, color photographs throughout
5¹/₂ x 7 inches

"This book is for painters who might question the stability of conventional artists' materials."

December 1984
34

December 1984
35

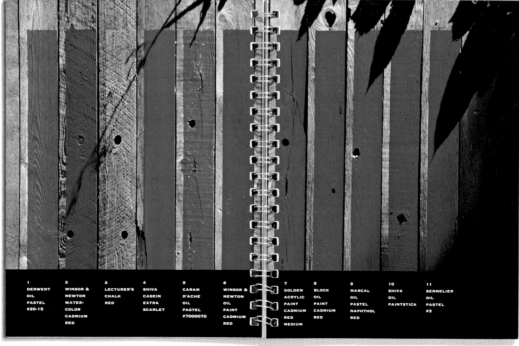

1	2	3	4	5	6	7	8	9	10	11
DERWENT	WINSOR &	LECTURER'S	SHIVA	CARAN	WINSOR &	GOLDEN	BLOCK	MARCAL	SHIVA	SENNELIER
OIL	NEWTON	CHALK	CASEIN	D'ACHE	NEWTON	ACRYLIC	OIL	OIL	OIL	OIL
PASTEL	WATER-	RED	EXTRA	OIL	OIL	PAINT	PAINT	PASTEL	PAINTSTICK	PASTEL
#20-15	COLOR		SCARLET	PASTEL	PAINT	CADMIUM	CADMIUM	NAPHTHOL		#3
	CADMIUM			#7000070	CADMIUM	RED	RED	RED		
	RED				RED	MEDIUM				

Time and Materials, 1994
100 pages, color photographs throughout
5¹/₂ x 7 inches

Cover: watercolor, acrylic, and casein on roofing felt.
Painted during rainfall and weathered outdoors for six
months, late summer, 1994, Tacoma, Washington.

With the exception of the drawing in Backyard Walls
2, which is on Bond Street, all of these projects were
developed on West 16th Street in New York City.
Some of them are still in progress.

Liquitex Sennelier Marcal Winsor
paint oil oil Newton
Hansa pastel pastel oil
yellow #22 cadmium paint
yellow Winsor
yellow

November 1979

6

January 1983

7

January 1991

10

April 1992

11

Painted Sun Trails, 1994
76 pages, color photographs throughout
7 x 11 inches

"A schedule of shadows" for William Paterson
College in Wayne, New Jersey

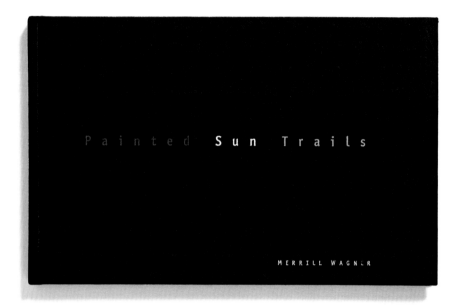

30

20

"The boulders are a time-keeping device, as shadows fill areas of color recorded in an earlier year at the same season and time of day. The photographs taken in each season make a schedule of shadows for anyone who sees the stones, either on site or in this book."

A small squarish patch of blue paint was added to describe the shadow on the second rock from the right.

31

Oil and Water, 1999
14 pages, accordian fold, color photographs throughout
8³/₄ x 13¹/₄ inches

In 1999 fourteen artists were invited to make site-specific works for Footfalls, an annual summer exhibition in Greenport, Long Island, New York.

The site for my project is at the end of Fourth Street in Greenport, where the village placed five boulders to prevent cars from driving into the

harbor. Several shadows moving across the stones between 7:00 am and 5:00 pm were painted during the week of the summer solstice in June.

The fixed paint and the moving shadows were then photographed throughout the day to make this timetable.   MERRILL WAGNER

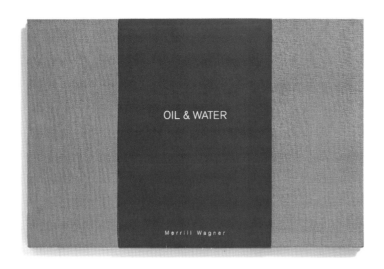

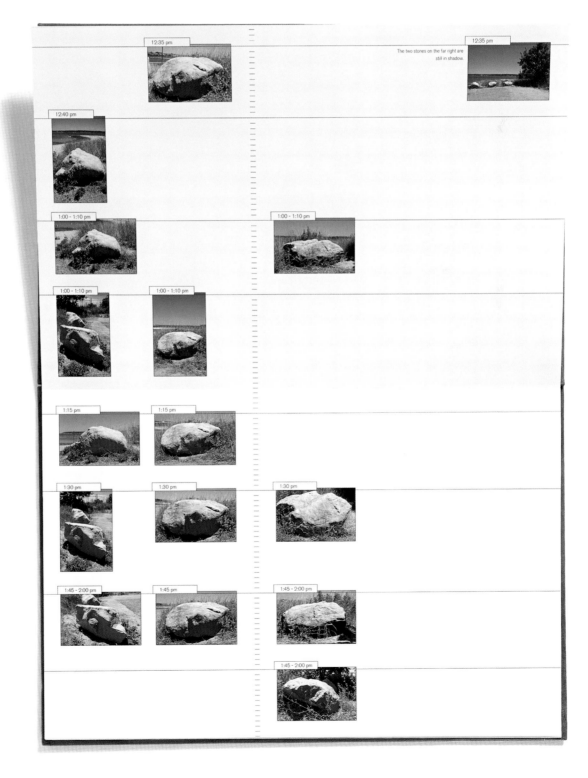

Self Portrait, 1960
Oil on linen
16 x 16 inches

Visually New York City is full of straight lines and gray colors. My first large-scale canvas paintings were full of straight lines and the memory of West Coast landscape images.

Still Life, 1960
Oil on linen
40 x 45 inches

Construction Site, 1961
Oil on linen
16 x 24 inches

Central Park, NYC, 1961–62
Oil on linen
20 x 24 inches

Central Park, NYC, 1961–62
Oil on linen
20 x 24 inches

Untitled, 1964
Acrylic on canvas
6 x 6 feet

studio view:
New York City, 1964

Untitled, 1965
Liquitex on linen
8 x 8 feet

studio view:
New York City, 1965

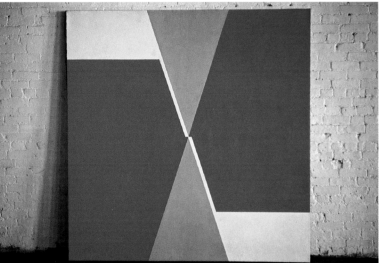
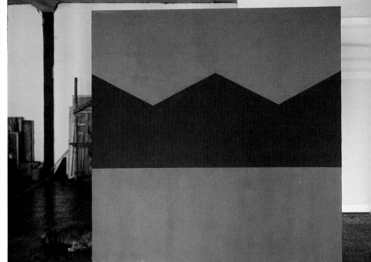

Untitled, 1966
Acrylic on canvas
6 x 6 feet

studio view:
New York City, 1966

Untitled, 1966
Liquitex on linen
8 x 8 feet

studio view:
New York City, 1966

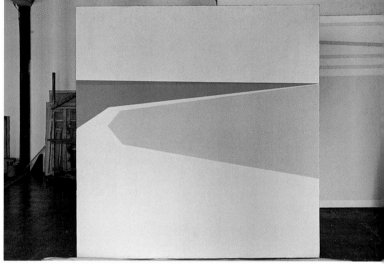

Untitled, 1966
Acrylic on canvas
6 x 6 feet

studio view:
New York City, 1966

Untitled, 1966
Liquitex on linen
8 x 8 feet

studio view:
New York City, 1966

Untitled, 1969
Acrylic on canvas
6 x 6 feet

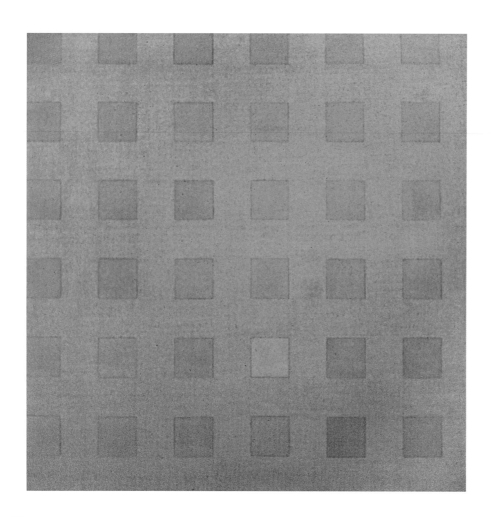

Clear Landing, 1999
Transparent tape
Project Studios 1 (PS 1), 3rd Floor
Long Island City, New York
(after Stairway landing renovation, 1999)

Installation View
Green Landing, 1978
Green gaffers tape, pastel, oil pastel
12 x 12 feet
Institute for Art and Urban Resources
Project Studios 1 (PS 1), 3rd Floor
Long Island City, New York

I had been making large acrylic paintings on linen using tape to mask off areas I wanted left unpainted. I liked the spontaneous look of the painting before the tape was removed, and began using the tape itself to make drawings, paintings, and prints.

Untitled, 1975
Masking tape, paper, pencil
11 x 14 inches

Untitled, 1975
Masking tape, paper, pencil
11 x 14 inches

Spanaway, 1979
Pastel on slate with one print on tape and Plexiglas
10 x 10 inches each

Untitled (Triptych), 1977
Conté crayon on tape, with two prints of Plexiglas and tape
24 x 18 inches each

 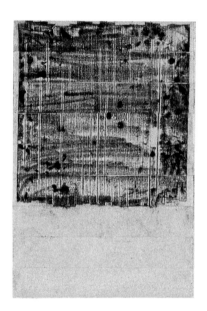 

Lakewolde, 1979
Oil paint on tape and Plexiglas
49 x 96 inches

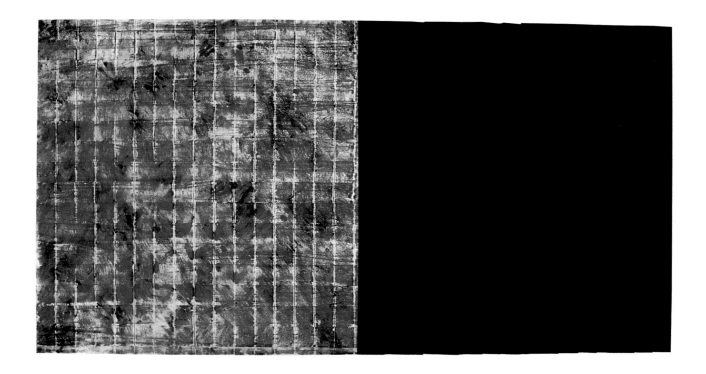

Untitled, 1977
Conté crayon on tape, one print on Plexiglas and tape
18 x 24 inches each

 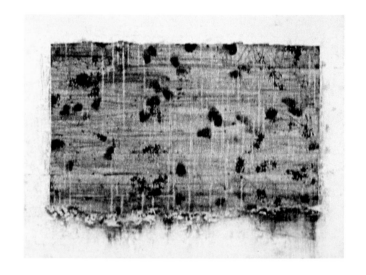

Puyallup, 1979
Pastel on slate with two prints on tape and Plexiglas
14$^1/_2$ x 30 inches each

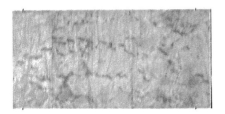 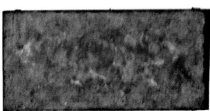 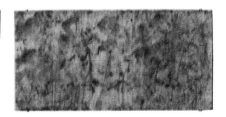

Shepherd's Crook, 1986
Watercolor, oil, acrylic on slate and soapstone
86 x 166 inches

Often I feel the need to order both the steel and the slate paintings through a simple geometry such as finding a square or other shape on the surface I am working on. I look for individual marks, blemishes, and colors in these materials that can be part of the work.

Hill, 1997–2001
Oil pastel on slate
42 × 92 inches

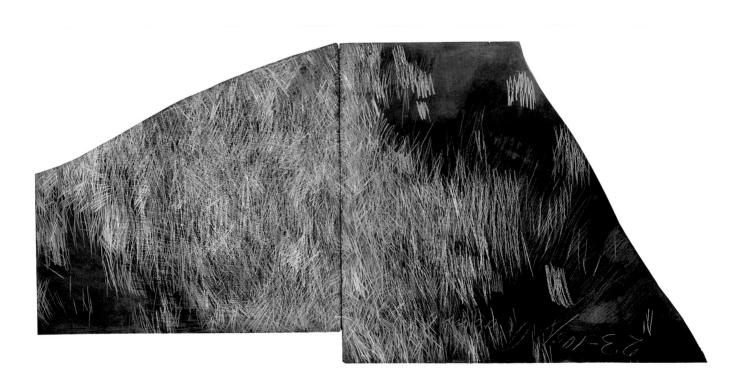

East Brunswick, 1989
Oil pastel on slate
80 x 106 inches

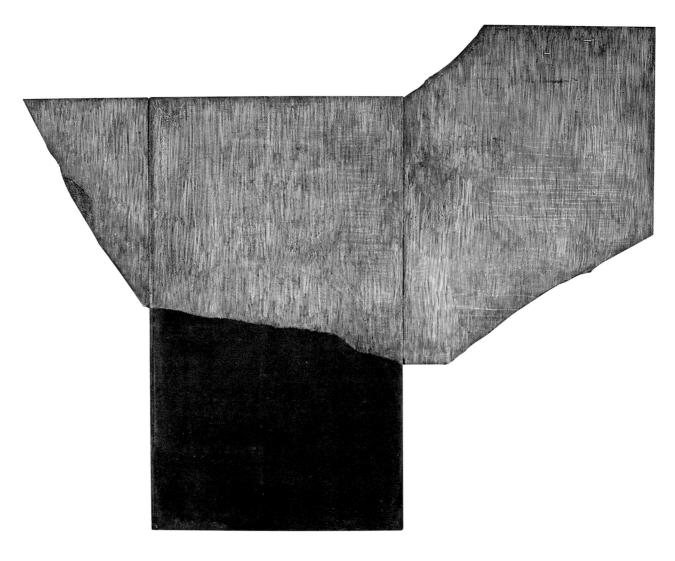

Line Drawing, 1987
Oil pastel on slate
7 x 13 feet

Cat's Cradle, 1989
Oil pastel, sewing thread, sewing hooks on slate
42 x 69 inches

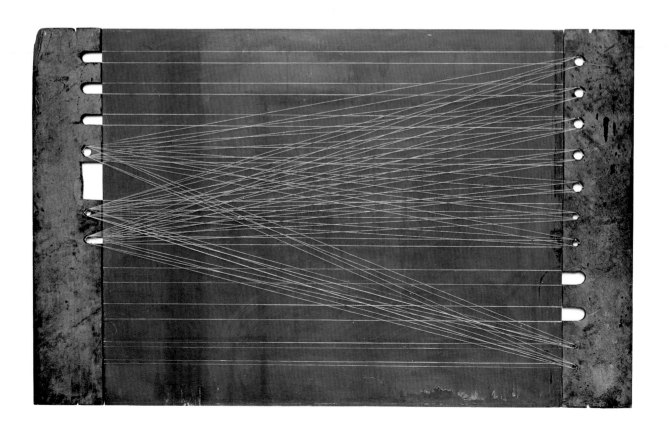

Revisions, 1982
Oil pastel on slate
79 x 72 inches

Installation view:

Stout's Lane, 1996
52¹/₂ x 216 inches
Springs Mills Company
New York City

Signal, 1986
Acrylic and watercolor on slate
42 x 134 inches

Indian Red, 1989
Oil on slate
20$^{1}/_{2}$ x 18 inches

Pysht, 1979
Oil crayon on slate
8 x 14 inches

Notations, 1996
Installation at Brandeis University (work in progress)

The contours of a hill go a certain way. And I got to be painting over and over again the contour of the hills. And some of the floor pieces on slate or stone are about gardens. When I'm painting, I think about terrain. I was doing paintings like that a lot in the '80s. Piles of stones with geometric marks. If you look at terrain, you can often see an organization—or you can find an organization that might be interesting.

Crossing #2, 1996
Oil pastel, marble
2 × 5 × 1 1/2 feet

Two Dogs Running in Opposite Directions #2, 1999
Oil pastel, stone
48 x 13 x 1 inches

Terrain #2, 1985
Oil on stone
17 x 64 x 36 inches

Marker, 1987
Oil on stone
14 x 34 x 50 inches

Untitled, 1997
Oil paint and graphite on marble
30 x 48 inches

Notations, 1996
Installation at Brandeis University (work in progress)

Palette, 2000
Oil on stone
47 x 57 x ¹/₂ inches

Pink Painting, 1999
Oil on stone
2 x 14 x 12 inches

Strawberry, 1999
Oil on stone
11¹/₂ x 14 x 2¹/₂ inches

Installation, 2000
Nicolaysen Museum of Art
and Discovery Center
Casper, Wyoming

The hillside looks different every minute. It's always changing. And certain aspects of nature, such as flowers, are intimate. You can pick them. And they're temporary. But if you look at the ocean, or if you go to the desert, you can't influence it in any way. It doesn't care about you. You just have to be there as a little observer. If you go up a mountain, you might witness a landslide or avalanche far away. I think that the larger paintings, the steel paintings, are more about that kind of experience.

Commencement Bay, 1994
Rust-Oleum on steel
96 x 96 inches

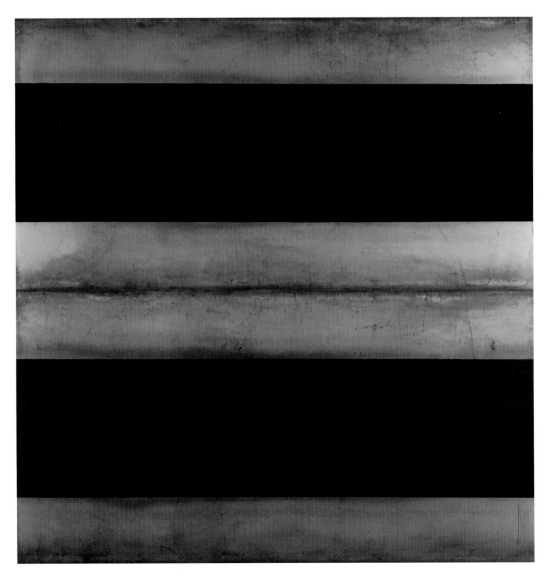

Omission, 2001
Rust-preventive paints on steel
120 x 97 inches

Untitled, 1989
Rust-Oleum on steel
20 x 20^1/$_2$ inches

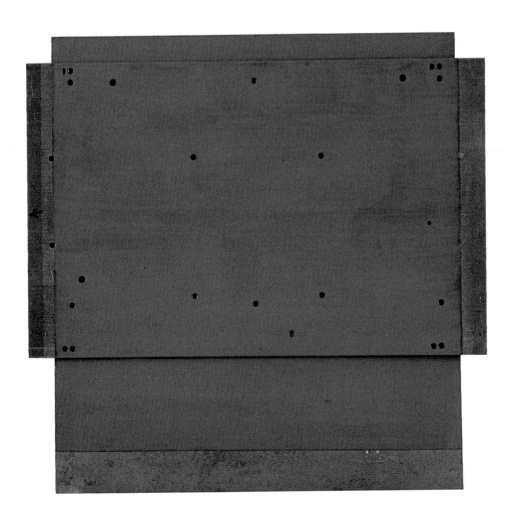

March, 1998
Rust-Oleum on steel
8 x 5 feet

Skid, 2001
Rust-preventive paints on steel
59 x 120 inches

Strait, 1993
Rust-Oleum on steel
48 x 57 inches

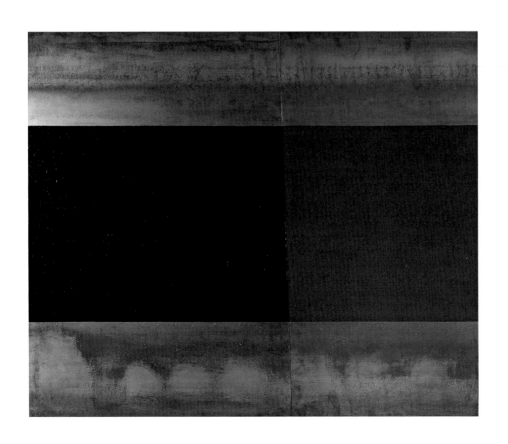

Plain, 1992
Rust-Oleum on hot-rolled steel
96 x 96 inches

Swing, 2001
Rust-preventive paints on steel
42 1/2 x 52 inches

Slide, 2000
Rust-preventive paints on steel
21 x 22 inches

Spring Painting, 2000
Rust-preventive paints on steel
18 x 18 inches

Untitled, 2001
Rust-preventive paints on steel
6¹/₂ x 26¹/₂ inches

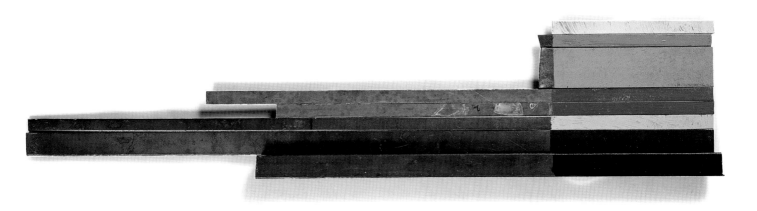

Installation, 2002
Kittredge Gallery
University of Puget Sound
Tacoma, Washington

The work is seasonal. Every season, I do what's there at the time. In March and April I paint forsythia for three weeks and so there's always three weeks of forsythia paintings. And then bushes in the summer. Now I'm painting flowers. In July, I always paint flowers. I paint these because I look out the window, and there they are.

August #13, 1998
Oil on linen
10 x 14 inches

May #8, 2000
Oil on linen
18¹/₈ x 15¹/₈ inches

#18, 2001
Oil on linen
9 x 10 inches

October #17, 1998
Oil on linen
14 x 10 inches

Installation, 2002
Kittredge Gallery
University of Puget Sound
Tacoma, Washington

March #3, 1998
Oil on linen
14 x 10 inches

October #16, 1998
Oil on linen
12 x 12 inches

#21, 1999
Oil on linen
18 x 12 inches

#22, 1999
Oil on linen
14 x 18 inches

1

2

Et Ego in Arcadia: Twenty Views

It is vain to dream of a wildness distant from ourselves.
—*Henry David Thoreau*

Lilly Wei

1

Merrill Wagner's studio takes up the entire first two floors of the historic brownstone in lower Manhattan where she has lived for many years, sharing it with her husband, Robert Ryman, their sons, Will and Cordy, and Robert's older son, Ethan, as well as a menagerie of pets. Now, since the children have grown up and moved out, she shares it with Robert, their parrot, dog, and two cats. You walk up the wide outer steps to enter a spacious, well-proportioned foyer edged by a gracefully turned staircase that invites you to climb upward to the living area, with its elegant, idiosyncratic clutter, evidence of richly lived, variegated lives. Downstairs, in the foyer, life also prevails: a rack of many coats, shoes, boots, a tangle of scarves, hats, gloves, bicycles, boxes of papers, scattered shopping bags, and more, much more tucked in corners, under the stairs. You would not call this by any means an empty nest. Once you enter the studio, however, it's another world, although equally overwhelmed. Here, almost everything pertains to art and to a lifetime spent in the arts. Wagner, who came to New York in the late 1950s after graduating from Sarah Lawrence College, maintains an establishment that, despite the solid grandeur of the architecture and furnishings, has the helter-skelter insouciance of bohemia, in spirit reminiscent of a graduate student's rambling, overflowing premises. There is art everywhere: upstairs, by family and friends; downstairs, almost all of it by Wagner. In her studio, on walls and floors, you can see the range of her materials and forms: immense steel paintings, painted rocks and pavement fragments, paintings on marble, slate constructions, recent landscapes on canvas, and tape pieces all jostle each other in easy camaraderie.

2

There is a pair of paint-splattered work boots in the middle of the studio that you step over. You step carefully in order not to cause an avalanche of papers or trip over some rocks. The studio's back wall is largely glass and on the ground level opens out onto a walled courtyard—a city backyard, a pocket landscape—bare at the end of winter. On the higher portions of a right-angled abutment, part of the wall at its northeast corner, a faint blue still clings to some of the bricks. It was first painted in November 1978: three rows of cobalt blue, three rows of cadmium yellow in oil pastel, paint powders, and soft pastels. Wagner photographed it at set intervals, documenting the uneven fading of the colors. Much of it has disappeared over the course of time. Along another wall are blistered traces of yellow from 1979; Wagner had painted four vertical rectangles in four manufacturers' brands of yellow in acrylic, oil pastel, and oil paint. Wagner also painted site-specific squares

3

4

5

or rectangles, always in primary colors, always varying shade, medium, and manufacturer, on other sections of the backyard walls, as well as on the brownstone's roof, skylight, and chimney. All were photographed at different intervals to see how they were faring, how the collaboration between nature and art was progressing. Some of the paintings changed colors, faded quickly, or were washed away, lasting only a short period, while others lingered on for more than twenty years, if only as traces, as remembrances of time past. These projects were documented in a book Wagner published in 1994 called *Time and Materials* (see pp. 18–19).

3

Wagner explored this same interaction of time, weather, and materials in other projects, published in books such as the earlier *Notes on Paint* (see pp. 16–17), dedicated to "painters who might question the stability of conventional artists' materials"; its terse entries read like those logged by an observant, dispassionate scientist.

4

Wagner also printed a calendar spanning the sixteen months from September 1982 through December 1983 that recorded the fate of six yellow rectangles painted just below the previous year's high-water mark on a cedar fence planted in the waters of Gravelly Lake in Tacoma. As part of these ventures—which are ongoing—she painted her Tacoma fence with large circles in 2000. Wagner gives plein air painting literal meaning. Locating her work outdoors, placing it directly into the landscape and leaving it there, she redefines landscape painting. It is ultimately a gallant and quixotic gesture, the willful act of an artist who wants to make her mark on nature while soliciting nature's active participation. Knowing these gestures are transient, she wants to know much more precisely how transient they are.

5

Seeing some pieces of slate on the floor, I remember the first time I saw Wagner's work. It was in the early '80s, at John Gibson's gallery. The impression remains strong even if the details are inexact. This is what I recall. There was a long low line of broken slate fragments set next to each other on the floor around the gallery, propped against the wall. Some were rounded, some sharp and jagged, some painted a brilliant cobalt blue, some black, some gray, left untreated. Nothing could have been simpler, yet the installation was extraordinarily vivid.

6

7

It was succinct, concentrated, stripped bare, simultaneously pragmatic and sublime. Formally, they were clearly pieces of slate, yet they were also a soaring mountain range in which scale was elastic, expanding as you contemplated their peaks and valleys and relationship to the inky economies of Chinese and Japanese landscape paintings and their uncanny ability to compress the vastness of the world into a certain number of feet.

6

Wagner often buys quantities of slate, stone, and metal. In 1980 she accepted an offer of all the slate blackboards discarded by a public school and stored them in her basement. She had used slate before, but now and for the next several years it became her primary material. These works varied in size and shape: some were small, others large, some regular, others broken. She would put the slate together in different combinations, influenced at times by the work of Sol LeWitt and Robert Mangold. Wagner would also draw on its surface in chalk in ways that recalled Cy Twombly. Others were painted or colored with pastels. Some recent slate works are thick with short, quick strokes, like a flurry of snow or other kinds of weather. Wagner, who has always been interested in materials and process, had stopped making conventional canvas paintings in the early '70s. Her abstract landscapes of the '70s became less and less referential in the '80s, yet landscape connotations remained, encoded in the organization of the geometry.

7

Wagner spent her first twenty years in the Pacific Northwest, in Tacoma and Olympia, Washington. Even now, she returns every summer. She says that she "is very moved by the landscape there. One could waken in the morning and, if it were a clear day, a huge snowcapped mountain could be seen from the windows of our house, which was at sea level. But the days are not always clear. It is often cloudy, foggy, or rainy, so the beauty of the mountain should never be taken for granted. When it appears, it is always a gift. Many people in the Northwest grow to know the mountains well."

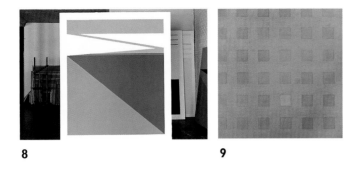

8

9

10

8

When asked what she had particularly liked that had been written about her work, she gave me this to read. "The ingredients of her paintings are the sky, distant trees, earth or grass and a road. Once one recognizes these objects, which may take a few moments because this is pure geometry, one is already projecting volume into what is actually flatness. The basic laws of linear perspective do the rest. Wagner's ability to convey a mood—these landscape views are examples of the 'great American loneliness'—with such sparse, unadorned shapes is remarkable" (Gordon Brown, *Arts Magazine,* Summer 1971).

9

Inspired in part by Eva Hesse, "in the late '60s," Wagner says, "I began thinking more about the materials that I had been using: linen or cotton canvas, paint, tape. I experimented with bare canvas in sections of the paintings. I made paintings the color of the linen, leaving some of the canvas unpainted, hoping to confuse people. Some of the paintings had alternating strips of painted and unpainted linen." For each new batch of strips, she would try to match the color of the unpainted linen, which would be constantly changing during the day as the light fluctuated. At night, the electric lights she used also altered the color of the linen. From the beginning, these kinds of subtle, often unremarked changes—this tracking of time through light, through gradations in colors as the light brightened and dimmed—intrigued her. She was a hunter, stalking the ephemeral effect, seizing and making an image of it.

10

"In the '70s," she says, "I continued to think about materials and ways of making paintings. I had been making large acrylic paintings on linen using tape to mask off areas I wanted left unpainted. I liked the look of the painting before the tape was removed. It was more spontaneous and free…so I made a series of paintings leaving the tape in place. I became interested in the tape itself." She used different color tapes and looked for different supports; glass, Plexiglas, slate, and marble seemed better than linen for her purposes. She would also make drawings, press tape strips over them, then carefully remove the strips one at a time and transfer them to glass or Plexiglas. You could see the print of the drawing through the transparent surfaces.

11

12

13

11

Then there are the rocks, mentioned above. Her studio is similar to an archaeological site. It holds a history of her art making as well as a projection for its future. The rocks are yet another aspect of her work, but they share the theme of her other outdoor pieces: measuring time through change. She paints rocks that she has found, in fields and on the streets, smooth-surfaced, pocked, and roughened shards. Often, she paints them in situ, like at William Paterson College in New Jersey, where she was invited to paint some boulders and smaller stones that had been unearthed during a renovation. She began this project in the fall of 1994. Again using primary colors, she painted shadows that appeared on the rocks, racing to capture a specific configuration before it moved and became another one. She painted for weeks, then photographed the results. She would record the time of day, the shadow, and the painted area, beginning in the morning and working until the sun went down. She repeated this process—which has performative aspects—during the winter solstice, the vernal equinox, and the summer solstice. In the fall of 1995 and again at the start of each new season, she photographed the shadows of the previous year, as fixed by the paint, and compared them to the shadows of a year later. It was a clock of sorts, a visualization of time, an antidote, for the moment, to its inevitable passage. Out of this, Wagner made another book, *Painted Sun Trails* (see pp. 20–21), where, seen in close-ups, the mild suburban boulders often assume the hauteur of her beloved Pacific peaks.

12

A similar project, but less intensive, was executed for *Footfalls,* the annual summer exhibition that takes place in Greenport, Long Island. Wagner painted in blue the shadows of five boulders and photographed them for a day, from 7 a.m. to 5 p.m., recording her findings in her latest book, *Oil and Water* (see pp. 22–23).

13

Wagner's installations of stones can resemble three-dimensional puzzles. Painting colors, drawing lines, and marking the surface with open circles, triangles, and other shapes, she connects the fractured surface by patterns that also help in reassembling the pieces. You imagine they might be mappings, arcane codes, commemorative markers, part of lost rituals or calculating devices and related to the ruins of Neolithic stone cultures. One she calls

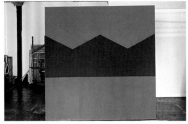

14

15

16

Palette (see p. 64), daubed with bright colors. Others are the multipart construction *Marker* (see p. 61) and the whimsical *Two Dogs Running in Opposite Directions #2* (see p. 59), a semi-circular arrangement of a half dozen flat stone fragments crossed by two chalk lines that continue onto the floor. Aided by the title, you see in the pieces two canines backing into each other.

14

Everyone has a landscape that defines them, that moves them intensely, that is their ideal of earthly beauty. For Wagner, it is the Northwest and its crystalline spaciousness, its spare wildness. She says as you become familiar with its higher terrains and elevations, the sudden changes in weather, the unexpected landslides and earthquakes, you realize the latent power of the mountains, which can abruptly, catastrophically erupt. It is a dangerous beauty, a hurtful, disdainful beauty that attracts artists of a certain temperament. Many people, Wagner says, become artists because they want to create beauty.

15

"New York is full of straight lines, rectangles and shades of gray. Some of my first large-scale canvas paintings were full of straight lines but also remembered West Coast landscape images," she says. This opposition of the urban and pastoral traditions and the tension that it creates is another ongoing theme in Wagner's work, which exists at the intersection of geometry and nature. It is a polarity evident from the beginning, as if the landscape needed to be contained, structured within the formal shapes of the geometric, the artificialities of colors that do not mirror nature, of white and black and gray, of materials that veer between the natural and the man-made, where each refers to the other. Sometimes when she applies short linear strokes to a surface she is working on, she thinks of grasses or rain. In the early '60s, when she returned to Washington during the summers, she was sur-prised that she couldn't make landscapes there as she could in Central Park; she couldn't make easel paintings. "The trees were too tall, the scene too enormous," she recollected. She needed to order that enormity somehow.

16

One way to order the wilderness was to organize it around simple geometries. Wagner says, "I try to find a square or other shape in the surfaces I am working on. I look for marks, blemishes, and color in these materials that can be part of the work." Her steel paintings of the '90s seem to contain fewer allusions to the natural world than do her

17   18

recent ones, which refer to landscape more overtly, but they, like all her work, are based
on some semblance of landscape, some response to it. Often quite large—painted with
industrial rust-preventive paints and primers in shiny and matte blacks, grays, cobalts, cop-
pery reds, rusty reds, and bright orange reds—they are frequently divided into zones, cut
by multiple horizon lines within which a sloping shape may loom, like a mountain rising
from a lake. At times, the form is doubled to suggest a reflection in water, as in *Memory*
(2000). It's big sky meeting big mountains and flat plains, flat rivers, lakes, and ocean. *Three
Red Primers* (1998–99) looks like an incinerated western sky, ruddy band after band glow-
ing, while the modulated darks of *Untitled Steel* (1998) are reminiscent of the ascending
zones of a night vista, silent, empty, endless. Wagner also combines steel plates of different
sizes and shapes, setting them at oblique angles to each other. Some have stacked narrow
strips of different lengths that create an unevenly pronged profile along one edge.

17

On the wall in one corner of the lower studio, there is a luxuriant, lilting abstraction.
Painted on glimmering white marble, it is a jumble of reds and pinks, of fat strokes and thin,
like a summer garden in full bloom. It was painted in 1995, a companion to some of the
representational landscapes that Wagner has begun to paint again: wild flowers in summer
bloom, snow-laden and icy branches of trees, the sunlit blaze of forsythia, the glow of
autumn foliage. For the last seven years, she has been going regularly to the country for
part of the week and painting what she sees around her house in Pennsylvania, its gentler
views superimposed over the rugged, more abstract terrain of Washington State. She likes
to "work with what's there." When Wagner first lived in New York, she studied the figure,
still life, and landscape at the Art Students League. "Off and on," she says, "I have continued
to paint from what I see."

18

Wagner also made a series of copper plates in 1996–97, called *Copper Drawings,* in collaboration with Garner Tullis. Employing recalcitrant dye grinders and dental drills, she
scored the surface with scribbled strokes and slashes that nonetheless look quick, as if
she were, once more, racing against time. The copper, burnished to brilliance, scintillates
like a constellated night sky, a white-lighted, shimmering vision of flux. Tullis, in a reversal,
asked Wagner to show the plates rather than the prints. Off and on, she has also made
collages and constructions that reveal her impulse to explore the diversity of materials.

19

19

Wagner has collaborated twice with the dancer Molissa Fenley. For *Weathering* (2000) she designed a stage environment using leftover scraps of linen that she had collected and left outside to weather. Later she bundled these strips together or hung them. Among other themes, the dance represented time, the time absorbed by the dancers and the time absorbed by the materials. In her other collaboration with Fenley, *331 Steps* (2002), Wagner used long sashes to suggest a kind of limitation. They were attached to the dancers and affixed to the back of the stage. Stones painted blue, yellow, and beige matched the costumes; placed discreetly, they made a pattern on the floor of the stage. Both collaborations are variants of Wagner's continuing endeavor to mark space and time.

20

Wagner's progression is not linear but cyclical. She works on many kinds of projects successively or simultaneously, a kind of eternal return to materials and methods that, once introduced into her vocabulary, are used over and over again in other permutations, steadily and tenaciously pushing her themes of mutuality and opposition further: urban and pastoral, abstract and representational, art and nature, order and disorder, time and memory, past and present, and what is lost and what remains, as a snowcapped mountain remains but its surface is constantly renewed, reconciled. It is an investment in small changes that add up, its tally prodigious and eloquent. Wagner, in her fifty years of art making, has been pursuing her particular dream of an American landscape, of some imagined beauty. "Yes," she says, "I set out to paint what I see in nature, but it's not possible to do. I know that now."

Lilly Wei is a New York–based critic and curator.

Installation, 1997, Tacoma Art Museum, Tacoma, Washington

Merrill Wagner

Born: Seattle, Washington, 1935

Education: Sarah Lawrence College, Bronxville, New York,
B. A. 1957, Art Students League, 1959–63

ONE-PERSON EXHIBITIONS

2002
University of Puget Sound, Kitteridge Gallery, Tacoma, WA
Stark Gallery, NYC
Art Resources Transfer, Inc., NYC
Larry Becker Contemporary Art, Philadelphia, PA
William Traver Gallery, Seattle, WA

2001
University of Wyoming, Art Museum, Laramie, WY
William Traver Gallery, Seattle, WA

2000
Freedman Gallery, Albright College Center for the Arts,
    Reading, PA
The Nicolaysen Art Museum, Casper, WY

1999
William Traver Gallery, Seattle, WA
Larry Becker Contemporary Art, Philadelphia, PA

1998
"Copper Drawings," Garner Tullis Workshop, NYC
P.S. 1 Institute for Art and Urban Resources, Long Island City,
    NY: "Green Landing Renovation"

1997
Rose Art Museum, Brandeis University, Waltham, MA
    (cat./traveling)
Tacoma Art Museum, Tacoma, WA (cat./traveling)
William Traver Gallery, Seattle, WA

1996
William Traver Gallery, Seattle, WA
Ben Shahn Gallery, William Paterson College, Wayne, NJ
    (cat./traveling)

1995
Stark Gallery, NYC

1994
William Traver Gallery, Seattle, WA
Outdoor Installation: "Painted Sun Trails: Recorded Cast
    Shadows, October–November," William Paterson College,
    Wayne, NJ
The Sandpiper Gallery. Tacoma, WA

1993
Outdoor Painting: "Runaway RedYellowBlue," C.W. Post
    Campus, Long Island University, Brookville, NY
Fulcrum Gallery, NYC
Larry Becker Contemporary Art, Philadelphia, PA

1992
Stark Gallery, NYC

1991
Lenore Gray Gallery, Providence, RI
Traver Gallery, Seattle, WA
Gemeentemuseum, The Hague, Holland
Galerie L'A, Liege, Belgium

1990
Larry Becker, Philadelphia, PA

1989
Julian Pretto Gallery, NYC
Fawbush Gallery, NYC
Traver Sutton Gallery, Seattle, WA

1988
Julian Pretto Gallery, NYC

1987
Traver Sutton Gallery, Seattle, WA

1986
John Gibson Gallery, NYC

1985
The Costa Rican–North American Cultural Center,
    San Jose, Costa Rica; Julian Pretto, curator
Harris Samuel & Co., Miami, FL
The Sandpiper Gallery, Tacoma, WA

1984
Tacoma Art Museum, Tacoma, WA
Ben Shahn Gallery, William Patterson College,
    Wayne, NJ

1982
Watson/de Nagy Gallery, Houston, TX
Harm Bouckaert Gallery, NYC
Charles Wright Academy, Tacoma, WA
Annie Wright School, Tacoma, WA

1981
David Bellman Gallery, Toronto, Ontario
Foster/White Gallery, Seattle, WA
Hal Bromm Gallery, NYC

1980
Outdoor Installation, 26 Bond Street, NYC
Tacoma Actor's Guild, Tacoma, WA

1979
The Clocktower, Institute for Art and Urban Resources, NYC
Hal Bromm Gallery, NYC

1978
P. S. 1, Institute for Art and Urban Resources,
    Long Island City, NY
Droll/Kolbert Gallery, NYC
Julian Pretto Gallery, NYC

1977
55 Mercer Gallery, NYC
Truman Gallery, NYC

1976
55 Mercer Gallery, NYC
55 Mercer Gallery, NYC

1974
55 Mercer Gallery, NYC

1971
55 Mercer Gallery, NYC
55 Mercer Gallery, NYC

1970
55 Mercer Gallery, NYC

SELECTED GROUP EXHIBITIONS

2002
"Site Specifics"; Carriage House, Islip Art Museum, East Islip,
    Long Island, NY
"Invitational Exhibition of Painting & Sculpture," American
    Academy of Arts & Letters, NYC
"25 Years of Painting"; Stark Gallery, NYC
"331 Steps," collaboration with Molissa Fenley,
    Joyce Theater, NYC

2001
"Ann Messner & Merrill Wagner," Lenore Gray Gallery,
    Providence, RI

2000
"Punk and Bloat," Molloy College Art Gallery,
    Rockville Center, Long Island, NY
"Abstract Painting," The Studio School, NYC
"(Un)resolved," Rosenberg and Kaufman Gallery, NYC
"Weathering," a collaboration with Molissa Fenley,
    The Kitchen, NYC
"Summer Invitational," Spencer Brownstone Gallery, NYC

1999
"Footfalls 1999," Site Specific Sculpture,
    Greenport, Long Island, NY
"Women and Geometric Abstraction," Pratt Institute, NYC
"Selections," Larry Becker Contemporary Art at Cherrystone
    Gallery, Wellfleet, Cape Cod, MA
"Planes of Color," Greg Kucera Gallery, Seattle, WA
"Judith Murray and Merrill Wagner," Simon Gallery,
    Morristown, NJ

1998
"Merrill Wagner & Scott Reynolds," Workspace Gallery, NYC
"The Tip of the Iceberg," Part III,
    Dorfman Projects/Art Resources Transfer
"Substance," Tricia Collins Contemporary Art, NYC
"Painting with an Edge: Four Contemporary Artists"
    Hunterdon Museum of Art, Clinton, NJ;
    Kristen Accola, curator.
"Paper +-" Dieu Donne Papermill, NYC, organized by
    Jackie Brody
"Hands on Color," Bellevue Art Museum. Belleview, WA

1997
"After the Fall," Snug Harbor Cultural Center, Staten Island,
    NY, Lilly Wei, curator (cat.)
"Drawing from Life," Stark Gallery, NYC
"Better Color through Chemistry," Islip Art Museum, East Islip,
    Long Island, NY

1995
"All about Edges," University of Rhode Island, Kingston, RI;
    J. Tolnick, curator
"Geometric Abstraction," C. Grimaldis Gallery, Baltimore, MD
"10 X 10: Artists Select a Painter of Their Choice,"
    New York Studio School, NYC
The Corcoran Gallery of Art 44th Biennial Exhibition of
    Contemporary American Painting: "Painting Outside
    Painting" (cat.)
"Julian's Show II," Littlejohn Contemporary Gallery, NYC;
    Julian Pretto, curator
"Alchemy," Proctor Art Center, Bard College,
    Annandale-on-Hudson, Harvey Quaytman, curator

1994

"Fashion in Metal; Metal in Art," Bergdorf Goodman, NYC

"Red, White Walls, & Blue," The Woodstock Guild's Kleinert Art Center, Woodstock, NY

"Tacoma Art Museum: Selections from the Northwest Collection," Seafirst Gallery, Seattle, WA

"Abstract Art In The Seattle Arts Commission Portable Works Collection," Seattle Center Pavillion, Seattle, WA

"Fallen Timber," Tacoma Art Museum, Tacoma, WA; Gregg Bell, curator

1993

"Impermanence. Andy Goldsworthy and Merrill Wagner," Aldrich Museum of Contemporary Art, Ridgefield, CT

"Silent Echoes," Tennisport Arts, Long Island City, NY; organized by Chris Haub

"Artists Select," Artists' Space, NYC

"Artists of the Aughts," Fulcrum Gallery, NYC

1992

"Breakdown!" Rose Art Museum, Brandeis University, Waltham, MA (cat.)

"Inaugural Show: Tennisport Arts," Long Island City, NY; organized by Chris Haub

1991

"Large Scale," Stark Gallery, NYC

"AIGA Book Show 1990," NYC

"Books as Art," Boca Raton Museum, Boca Raton, FL

1990

"Carl Affarian, Stephen Antonakos, Merrill Wagner," Fawbush Gallery, NYC

"Opening Invitational," Stark Gallery, NYC

1989

"Three Artists Who Work With Slate," E. L. Stark Gallery, NYC

"A Debate on Abstraction; The Persistence of Painting," The Bertha and Karl Leubsdorf Gallery, Hunter College, New York; Vincent Longo, curator (cat.)

"Plane Into Form," mezzanine, One World Trade Center, NYC; Barbara Valenta, curator, sponsored by the Organization for Independent Artists

"100 Drawings by Women," Hillwood Art Gallery, C. W. Post Campus, Long Island University; traveling through America and Europe (cat.)

"Celebrating the Permanent Collection," The Tacoma Art Museum, Tacoma, WA

"A Decade of Abstraction, 1979–1989," Seattle Center, Seattle, WA; Matthew Kangas, curator

1988

"The Legacy of Surrealism in Contemporary Art," The Ben Shahn Gallery, William Paterson College, Wayne, NJ (cat.)

"Out of Order," Anne Plumb Gallery, NYC; Christian Haub, curator

"Route 27," John Gibson Gallery, NYC

"A Living Tradition: Selections from the American Abstract Artists," The Bronx Museum of the Arts, traveling; Phillip Verre, curator (cat.)

"Seattle, Before and After," Center of Contemporary Art, Seattle, WA (cat.)

"The $1000 Show," John Davis Gallery, NYC

1987

"Seattle Sculpture 1927–1987," A Bumbershoot Visual Arts Exhibition, Seattle Center, Seattle, WA; Matthew Kangas, curator

"It's About Time," The New York City Gallery, Department of Cultural Affairs, NYC

"Jane Logemann and Merrill Wagner," Lenore Gray Gallery, Providence, RI

1986

"About Place: Contemporary American Landscape," Institute for Art and Urban Resources, Long Island City, NY (cat.)

"American Abstract Artists—50th Anniversary Celebration 1936–1986," The Bronx Museum of the Arts, NYC (cat.)

"Nancy Haynes, Suzanna Tanger, and Merrill Wagner," Kingsborough College, Brooklyn, NYC

"Slate," Springs Mills Industries, New York; curated by the Art Advisory Service, the Associate Council of the Museum of Modern Art, NYC

1985

"Color and Field," Roger Ramsay Gallery, Chicago, Il; Julian Pretto, curator

"Abstract Painting as Surface and Object," Hillwood Art Gallery, Long Island University, C. W. Post Campus (cat.)

"Abstract Painting," John Gibson Gallery, NYC

"Time Will Tell," Squibb International Headquarters, Princeton, NJ (cat.)

"Invitational," Condeso-Lawler Gallery, NYC; Tiffany Bell, curator

"Diversity—New York Artists," University of Rhode Island, Kingston, RI (cat.)

"Ten Years of Visual Arts at Princeton," Princeton, NJ (cat.)

1984–85

"Large Drawing," curated by Elke Solomon, Independent Curators Incorporated, traveling exhibition (cat.)

1984

"From the Abstract to the Image," Oscarsson Hood Gallery, NYC

"Installations," Directions of Broadway, NYC

"Artists Call," Terry Dintenfass Gallery, NYC

"American Women Artists, Part I," Sidney Janis Gallery, NYC (cat.)

"Fifteen Abstract Artists," Susan Montezinos Gallery, Philadelphia, PA

1983

"American Abstract Artists," Weatherspoon Art Gallery, Greensboro, NC, also at the University of Alabama (cat.)

"55 Mercer—12 Years," 55 Mercer Gallery, NYC, (cat.)

Group Exhibition, John Weber Gallery, NYC; Lucio Pozzi, curator (cat.)

"Works on Paper," Weatherspoon Art Gallery, Greensboro, NC; Donald Droll, curator (cat.)

"Christmas Show," Bonnier Gallery, NYC

"A More Store," Tilton Gallery, NYC

1982

"Recent Aspects of All Over," Harm Bouckaert Gallery, NYC; Theodore Bonin, curator

"Anti-Apocalypse; Artists' Response to Nuclear Peril," William Paterson College, Wayne, NJ

"Unpunctuated – New Papers," Grommet Gallery, NYC; Marcia Hafif and Jean Dupuy, curators

1981

"Painting About Painting," William Paterson College, Wayne, NJ (cat.)

"American Abstract Artists," Summit Art Center, Summit, NJ

Group Exhibition, Lowe Art Gallery, Hofstra University, Hempstead, NY (cat.)

"New Art II: Surfaces/Textures," Spring Penthouse Exhibition, Museum of Modern Art, NYC

"Heresies Benefit," Grey Art Gallery, New York University, NYC

Summer Group Exhibition, Hal Bromm Gallery, NYC

"Small Scale Works," Hal Bromm Gallery, NYC

"Drawings Selected by the Gallery Advisory Council," William Paterson College, Wayne, NJ (cat.)

1980

"One Grand Leap Year Art Sale," Franklin Furnace Gallery, NYC

"Painted Structures," Jeffrey Fuller Gallery, Philadelphia, PA

1979

"Drawing," Hal Bromm Gallery, NYC

Summer Group Exhibition, Young/Hoffman Gallery, Chicago, IL

"American Abstract Artists," Betty Parsons Gallery, NYC (cat.)

Group Exhibition, Julian Pretto Gallery, NYC

"Small Works," Young/Hoffman Gallery, Chicago, IL

"A Great Big Drawing Show," P. S. 1, Long Island City, NY

1978

"The Reality of Art," Truman Gallery, NYC

"Recent Works," Hal Bromm Gallery, NYC

"Post Minimal Artists," Nobe Gallery, NYC; Per Jensen, curator

1977

American Abstract Artists Exhibition, William Patterson College, Wayne, NJ

"Outside the City Limits," Thorpe Intermedia Gallery, Sparkill, NY (cat.)

Group Exhibition, Julian Pretto Gallery, NYC

"Christmas Show," Truman Gallery, NYC

Summer Group Exhibition, Droll/Kolbert Gallery, NYC

1976

American Abstract Artists Memorial Exhibition, Westbeth, NYC

1974

"55 Mercer Traveling Group Exhibition," Gallery Association of New York State (cat.)

1972

"Grids," Institute of Contemporary Art, University of Pennsylvania, Philadelphia, PA (cat.)

1971

"26 Contemporary Women Artists," Aldrich Museum of Contemporary Art, Ridgefield, CT (cat.)

"Christmas Show," Penthouse Gallery, The Museum of Modern Art, NYC

1970

55 Mercer Gallery, NYC

PUBLICATIONS BY THE ARTIST

2000

Oil and Water. Self-published. Hong Kong and Seattle, WA.

1996

Painted Sun Trails. Self-published. Hong Kong and Seattle, WA.

1994

Time and Materials. Self-published. Hong Kong and Seattle, WA.

1990

Notes on Paint. Self-published with funds from NEA Artists' Fellowship Grant. Seattle, WA.

1984

A Calender, September 1982–December 1983
Self-published. Seattle, WA.

PUBLIC COLLECTIONS

Bellevue Art Museum, Bellevue, WA
Charles Schwab Company, San Fransisco, CA
Chase Manhattan Bank, New York, NY
Coopers and Lybrand, Boston, MA
Gemeentemuseum, The Hague, Holland
Richard Gluckman, Architects, New York, NY
Goldman Sachs Company, New York, NY
Long Island University, Brookville, NY
Microsoft Corporation, Redmond, WA
Nicolaysen Art Museum, Casper, WY
Project Studios One, The Institute for Art and Urban
    Resources, Long Island City, NY
The Rose Art Museum, Brandeis University, Waltham, MA
Sears Merchandising, Chicago, IL
Seattle Arts Commission, Seattle, WA
Seattle First National Bank, Seattle, WA
Smith College, Northampton, MA
Tacoma Art Museum, Tacoma, WA
University Museum at Southern Illinois University,
    Edwardsville, IL
Weatherspoon Art Gallery at The University of North
    Carolina, Greensboro, NC
William Paterson College, Wayne, NJ

BIBLIOGRAPHY

2002

Anderson, Jack. "Dance Review; A Solo Influence in Group
    Works." *New York Times,* Jan.18.
Boyce, Roger. "Merrill Wagner at Stark." *Art in America,* Oct.,
    p. 159.
Hall, Emily. "Visual Art: Visual Silence." *The Stranger,* Apr. 11.

2001

Hackett, Regina. "What's on Display." *Seattle Post Intelligencer,*
    Feb. 19, p. 22.
Hoffberg, Judith. "Oil and Water by Merrill Wagner." *Umbrella* 24,
    no. 2 (Aug.), p. 51.
Princenthal, Nancy. Artists' Book Beat. *Art on Paper* 5, no. 3
    (Jan./Feb.), p. 95.
Wagonfeld, Judy. "New Paintings on Steel." Galleries at a Glance.
    [William Traver Gallery]. Jan. http://www.seattlesearch.com.

2000

Anderson, Jack. "With Movements Stepping to Flute, Cello and
    Silence." *New York Times,* Feb. 28, sec. E, p. 28.
Braff, Phyllis. "Punk and Bloat." Art Reviews. [Molloy College Art
    Gallery, Rockville Center, NY]. *New York Times,* Dec. 10,
    Long Island ed.
Hamilton, Judy. "Wagner Steels the Show." *Casper Star Tribune,*
    Feb. 17, sec. C, pp. 1–2.
Jowitt, Deborah. "Uncharted Terrain." *Village Voice,* Feb. 22.
Seidel, Miriam. "Merrill Wagner at Larry Becker Contemporary
    Art." *Art in America,* Apr., p. 160.

1999

Kangas, Matthew. *Sculpture Magazine* 18, no. 15, p. 63.
Schwabsky, Barry. "Abstract Introspection in 2 Distinct Styles."
    On the Town. *New York Times,* Oct. 31, New Jersey sec.,
    p. 13.
Sozanski, Edward J. "Rustoleum Never Sleeps." *Philadelphia
    Enquirer,* Nov. 12.

1998

Murdock, Robert. "Scott Reynolds and Merrill Wagner." *Review
    Magazine,* Apr. 1, p. 10.

1997

Clayton, Alec. Arts and Leisure. *Tacoma (WA) City Paper,* June
    26, p. 4.
Hackett, Regina. *Seattle Post Intelligencer,* June 17, pp. C1, C3.
Kangas, Matthew. Tempo. *Seattle Times,* July 3, p. C22.
Princenthal, Nancy. Artists' Book Beat. *On Paper* 1, no. 5
    (May/June), pp. 43–44.
Wagonfeld, Judy. *Tacoma Weekly,* vol. 7, issue 25, July 10–17,
    pp. 4–5.

1996

Dorsey, John. "Too Much 'Different' Makes Show Uneven."
    Baltimore Sun, Jan. 14, Arts sec. K, p. 1.
Hackett, Regina. "What's Happening." *Seattle Post Intelligencer,*
    May 24, p. 15.
Heartney, Eleanor. "Merrill Wagner at Stark." *Art in America,*
    Apr., p. 115.
Schwabsky, Barry. "Three Painters Add a Human Touch to
    Abstraction." On the Town. *New York Times,* Sept. 22,
    New Jersey sec., p. 14.
Watkins, Eileen. "Artistic Trio's Exhibition Targets the Natures
    of Time and Space." *Newark Sunday Star Ledger,*
    October 6, sec. 4, p. 10.

1995

Dorsey, John. "Grimaldis Abstract Show in Beautiful Shape."
    Baltimore Sun, May 12.
McLennan, Douglas. "Art Walk Includes Look at Recent
    Museum Acquisitions." *Tacoma (WA) News Tribune,*
    Feb. 16, p. SL-11.
Princenthal, Nancy. Artists' Book Beat. *[Time and Materials.]*
    Print Collector's Newsletter 27, no. 2 (May–June), p. 71.
Van Siclin, Bill. "Geometric Art Crosses Line of Convention."
    Providence Journal Bulletin, Feb. 10, sec. D Lifebeat, p. P1.

1994

Hackett, Regina. "Painter Puts Her Signature on Lyrical
    Abstraction." *Seattle Post Intelligencer,* Mar. 23.
Kangas, Matthew. "Wagner, Flavin Make Most Out of Minimal
    Art." *Seattle Times,* Mar. 7, sec. F, p. 1.
Smith, Roberta. "Artists Select, Part 1." Art in Review. *New
    York Times,* Jan. 7, p. C23.

1993

Kangas, Matthew. "Late Modernist Painting in the Pacific
    Northwest." *Modernism and Beyond: Women Artists of the
    Pacific Northwest.* Edited by Laura Brunsman and Ruth
    Askey. New York, Midmarch Arts Press, p. 98.
Nathan, Jean. "Game, Set and Perspective." *New York Times,*
    May 16, Styles sec., p. 9.
Zimmer, William. "Industrial-Strength Sculpture with
    Economy-Size Politics." *New York Times,* Mar. 28,
    Connecticut ed.

1992

Bell, Tiffany. "Looking at Kelly's Paintings Now." *Artstudio* 24
    (spring), pp. 158–75.
Heartney, Eleanor. "Merrill Wagner at Stark." *Art in America,*
    Oct., p. 147.
Massera, Jean-Charles. "Merrill Wagner: Galerie L'A, Liege."
    Arte Factum, Feb.–Mar., p. 29.

1991

Heytig, Lien. NRC Handelsband (Holland), July 19.
Massera, Jean-Charles. "Merrill Wagner, Gemeentemuseum."
    La Haye. *Art Press,* Nov., p. 100.
Princenthal, Nancy. Artists' Book Beat. *[Notes on Paint].* *Print
    Collector's Newsletter* 21, no. 6 (Jan./Feb.), p. 237.

1990

Hoffberg, Judith. "Notes on Paint." *Umbrella* 13, no. 2 (Dec.),
    p. 45.
Rice, Robbin. "Cool Slate and Weathered Wood." *Philadelphia
    City Paper,* Mar. 15–23.

1989

Brunsman, Laura. "Decade of Abstraction: Expressionism." *The Arts Newsletter of the Kings County Arts Commission.*

Faust, Gretchen. "Merrill Wagner." *Arts Magazine*, Sept., p. 94.

Mathieson, Karen. "Artists Speak Vibrant Visual Language." *Seattle Times*, Nov. 23.

Nesbit, Lois. "Merrill Wagner: Fawbush Gallery." *Artforum*, Oct., p. 172.

Smith, Roberta. "Galleries Paint a Brighter Picture for Women." *New York Times*, Apr. 14, p. C29.

1988

Higuchi, Shoichiro. "Swimmer in the Stream of Time." *Idea* (Tokyo), Sept., p. 102.

Kangas, Matthew. "Banned in Puyallup." *Seattle Weekly*, Nov. 29.

Raynor, Vivien. "At the Ben Shahn, Surrealism's Legacy." *New York Times*, Feb. 21, p. 18.

1987

Hackett, Regina. "Paul Heald Paintings Line up a Spirited Struggle." *Seattle Post Intelligencer*, Nov. 16.

Kangas, Matthew. "Time Travellers." *Seattle Weekly*, Nov. 18, p. 45.

"Lenore Gray Gallery Shows Abstracts by New York Artists." *Antiques and the Arts Weekly* (Newtown, CT), Dec. 18, p. 101.

"News of the Print World: People and Place; American Abstract Artists, 50th Anniversary Print Portfolio 1987." *Print Collector's Newsletter*, May–June, p. 58.

1986

Bell, Tiffany. "Merrill Wagner." *Arts Magazine*, May, p. 100.

Brenson, Michael. "The Landscape Maintains Its Hold On American Artists." *New York Times*, Mar. 9, p. H33.

Henry, Gerrit. "Merrill Wagner at John Gibson." *Art in America*, Sept., p. 139.

1985

"Actual Exhibit at Squibb." *Trentonian* (NJ), June 4.

"Art." *Newark (NJ) Star-Ledger*, June 7.

Artner, Alan. "Color Field Painting Returns in an Impressive Exhibition." *Chicago Tribune*, Jan. 18, sec. 7, p. 10.

Bell, Jane. "Abstract Painting, John Gibson." *ARTnews*, Sept. p. 142.

Harrison, Helen. "Treating the Canvas as an Object in Its Own Right." *New York Times*, Mar. 3, Long Island ed.

Lyon, Christopher. *Chicago Sun-Times*, Jan. 18, p. 47.

Reynolds, Rosemary. "The Arts." *San Juan (Costa Rico) Tico Times*, Nov. 22.

Wallach, Amei. "Abstract Power." *Long Island (NY) Newsday*, Feb. 22.

Zimmer, William. "At Squibb: A Display of How Little Change There Really Is." *New York Times*, July 28.

1984

Donohoe, Victoria. "Is Abstract Painting Regaining Its Popularity?" *Philadelphia Inquirer*, Sept. 14.

Wotton, Warren. "Sticking to Roots, Wagner Charms New York." *Tacoma News Tribune*, Jan. 22.

1983

Glueck, Grace. "A Group Exhibition Curated by Lucio Pozzi." *New York Times*, July 8.

Westfall, Stephen. "Merrill Wagner/Peter Brown." *Arts Magazine*, Mar.

1982

Cohen, Joelle. "New York Art Scene Lured Away Tacoma's Merrill Wagner." *Tacoma News Tribune*, Aug. 8.

Feinberg, Andrew. "Picking Up the Pieces in a Tight Art Market." *Venture Magazine*, Dec., p. 42.

Glueck, Grace. "Group Show Celebrates Pollack Legacy in Art." *New York Times*, Sept. 10.

_____. "Merrill Wagner Works." *Tacoma News Tribune*, Sept. 17.

Westfall, Stephen. "Recent Aspects of Allover." *Arts Magazine*, Dec.

1981

Deschamp, Madeleine. *La Peinture Americaine, les mythes et la matiere.* Èd. Denoîl, p. 266.

Hafif, Marcia. "Getting on with Painting." *Art in America*, Apr.

Shirey, David. "Art Sampler." *New York Times*, Feb. 8.

Skoggard, Ross. "Merrill Wagner at Hal Broom." *Art in America*, May.

Watkins, Eileen. *Newark (NJ) Star-Ledger*, Jan. 25.

1979

Glueck, Grace. "Painting." *New York Times*, Dec. 24.

Russell, John. "Art." *New York Times*, Dec. 14.

Zimmer, William. "Installations." *Soho Weekly News*, Dec. 13.

1978

Bell, Tiffany. "Merrill Wagner." *Arts Magazine*, Jan.

Frank, Peter. "Schoolhouse Rock." *Village Voice*, May 18.

Lubell, Ellen. "Extensions of Form." *Soho Weekly News*, Dec. 13.

1976

Lubell, Ellen. "Merrill Wagner." *Arts Magazine*, June.

1974

Bell, Jane. "Grace Bakst Wapner and Merrill Wagner." *Arts Magazine*, June.

1972

Pincus-Witten, Robert. "Merrill Wagner." *Artforum*, Feb.

1971

Bowles, Jerry. "Merrill Wagner." *ARTnews*, summer issue.

Brown, Gordon. "55 Mercer." *Arts Magazine*, summer issue. Soho Statement 1, no. 1 (Nov.).

TEACHING POSITIONS

1993–98
Parsons School of Design, NYC

1986–93
Princeton University, Princeton, NJ

1985–86
University of Puget Sound, Tacoma, WA; summer sessions

1983–84
Princeton University, Princeton, NJ

Haags Gemeentemuseum installation, 1991
The Hague, The Netherlands